THE REAGAN CHRONICLES

A CARTOON CARNIVAL

BY

DWANE POWELL

EDITED BY STEVE ADAMS ■ WITH AN INTRODUCTION BY JEFF MacNELLY *published by*

Algonquin Books of Chapel Hill

Post Office Box 2225, Chapel Hill, North Carolina 27515-2225

in association with

Taylor Publishing Company

1550 West Mockingbird Lane, Dallas, Texas 75235

Design by Molly Renda.

Library of Congress Cataloging-in-Publication Data

Powell, Dwane.

The Reagan chronicles.

1. Reagan, Ronald—Caricatures and cartoons.

2. United States—Politics and government—1981– —

Caricatures and cartoons. 3. American wit and humor,

Pictorial. I. Adams, Steve. II. Title.

E877.2.P68 1987   973.927   87-14483

ISBN 0-912697-72-5

THE REAGAN CHRONICLES

ALGONQUIN BOOKS OF CHAPEL HILL ■ 1987

To my daughter Devon, age four,
whose generation will pick up the tab
for the Reagan years

CONTENTS

had just finished the pencil work, and was getting ready to ink in the next day's cartoon, when this guy in his late fifties burst through my door.

"I just want to tell you that that cartoon in today's paper stinks!" he shouted through frothing lips. Caught off guard, I let him ramble, hoping that he wouldn't reach for anything more deadly than a cigarette. After he cooled off a bit, I escorted him out of the building and went promptly to the guard desk to inquire how a live one had managed to slip through our freshly-installed, $100,000 security system.

Welcome to the world of lampooning Ronald Reagan. When Reagan was elected, I set out with a vengeance to mine what looked to be the great mother lode of cartoon fodder—a Grade B actor president, misstatement after misstatement, Laffer curves drawn on napkins representing national economic policy, and a staff straight out of Abbott and Costello.

It became immediately obvious that we weren't dealing with Jimmy Carter here. Now, when I ventured out to give talks, the Reagan cartoons were met with silence, followed by questions like "What gives you the right to do *that* to the President of the United States?"

Then the polls started coming in. Everyone loved the guy! So James Watt wanted to strip-mine the whole U.S.! So Anne Burford wanted a toxic waste dump in every back yard! So Ed Meese wanted to take the U.S. legal system back to the Middle Ages. "Stop picking on our Ron and join the bandwagon!" came the phone calls, letters, and walk-in guests. My wife Jan, who runs her own business and often negotiates important transactions, started telling clients her husband is an accountant.

So began the years of purgatory for the pundits. Spitting in the wind became more like spitting in a hurricane. Right wing zealots ran rampant, and smugly rubbed it in at every chance. Friends suggested that I stop picking on the goose that lays the golden BMW.

I lampooned James Watt. "Right on!" came the replies. I nailed Burford good. "Yeah, git th' wench!" Then I took a whack at the man whose policies Watt and Burford had been carrying out. My phone suddenly became hot to the touch.

"You Commie pinko anti-American ##%***!!##*!"

Then, one day hundreds of cartoonists', comedians', and columnists' careers were suddenly saved! Reagan was caught trading arms with the Ayatollah, the only person the American people hate as much as they like Reagan. Other revelations followed—money to the contras, secret funds, shredded documents, cover-ups, lies, etc. Closer examination revealed a president dangerously out of touch with his administration. "What did he know and when did he know it?" was soon replaced by "Does he know anything?"

Business attitudes that had taken root with the Reagan Revolution yielded a plethora of stock market scams and hostile takeovers. Mass exodus plagued the White House staff, and one of the main beneficiaries of the Reagan years, the Religious Right, was beset with allegations that a popular televangelist couldn't keep his britches up and had been flummoxing his flock. Still, it's doubtful that any of this would have stuck without the real glue—the fact that "Ron dealt with the Ayatollah?!!"

After eight years of trying to doodle down the administration that promised to have America standing tall again, I'm still looking through the morning paper for a morsel on which to base the next day's cartoon. The deficit is bigger than ever. Marines are letting Russian women tromp through our embassy. The trade imbalance is worsening. There are more homeless people than ever. A former top administration official is under indictment. Two more are seeking immunity. Farmers are going broke at an alarming rate. World opinion of the U.S. is at an all-time low.

So, I pick a topic and take another swipe at the old gipper. "This morning's cartoon was hilariously on target!" comes a reply. A thought passes through my mind. What's so damn funny?

DWANE POWELL
Raleigh, North Carolina

INTRODUCTION BY JEFF MacNELLY

Introducing Dwane Powell's stuff is like playing a piano prelude to a howitzer barrage. These things just don't need much introducing. Maybe I should just stand back and holler, "Duck!"

Dwane is doubly blessed in his profession. Not only does he possess a pure cartooning style, but he gets to perpetuate it in my favorite part of the planet. By "pure" I guess I mean *original,* but a Powell cartoon is also unhampered by pretensions and delusions of being fine art disguised as cartooning. You see, many of us in this line of work secretly believe we are fine artists—watercolorists, sculptors, banjo pickers, whatever. Dwane cheerfully admits that he never could do "serious" art. Never wanted to, although he does play a mean guitar.

What you've got here is 120 Proof cartooning which, being a product of the Old North State, has been cut rather liberally with a truckload of moonshine. It's the unrestrained goofiness of Powell's work that hits you first. But unlike many cartoonists, Dwane doesn't stop at the surface with merely a humorous comment on the news. His sense of humor, exaggeration, and caricature are far from sugar coating—they are the essential ingredients that supply the kick in the recipe.

Now, I have to explain that I wince about 92 percent of the time when I see a Powell cartoon. I mean, George Will in the sack with Reagan? Helms escorting Miss Constitution to a back alley abortion? Nancy reading Mrs. Woodrow Wilson's memoirs? Clearly these are all tasteless, biased slams at hapless victims, and they're drawn in a vicious, slashing, don't-give-a-damn style—exactly the way a cartoon should be.

Dwane approaches his subjects the way all great cartoonists should: from behind, doing 25 miles an hour over the speed limit, leaning on the horn. Rude, irritating, irresponsible—and very effective.

I may disagree with what he says from time to time, but I will defend to the death my right to enjoy his stuff over and over.

You too.

THE REAGAN CHRONICLES

I.
LADIES AND GENTLEMEN . . .

7/6/80 The Reagan Revolution begins: Reagan proposes to increase revenues by cutting taxes.

10/30/80 *Reagan gives a preview of things to come.*

12/24/80 Reagan begins putting foxes in charge of chicken coops — including James Watt at Interior.

1/21/81 Iran releases the hostages just as Reagan is sworn in,
denying Carter a last-minute triumph and giving the networks fits.

2/3/81 *It appears that wunderkind David Stockman is serious about budget cuts.*

3/19/81 Reagan's economic advisers promise that "safety net programs" will continue to protect the "truly needy."

3/29/81 Crisis management arises as an early theme—and Alexander Haig is miffed when George Bush is put in charge.

9

5/24/81 *A Miss America contestant is tossed out for padding her assets. Of course, beauty is in the eye of the beholder.*

7/5/81 Tip O'Neill wants to put up a fight, but conservative Democrats play roll-over on Reagan's economic package.

8/4/81 Reagan's three-year tax cut sails through Congress despite serious questions over where it will lead.

8/5/81 Air traffic controllers go on strike. Reagan fires 11,500.

13

9/6/81 Reagan's aides allow that they got along pretty well without the president during his 28-day vacation at the ranch.

14

10/23/81 *Leaders of 22 countries meet in a posh Mexican resort to discuss the problems of developing nations.*

10/24/81 *The conservative Wildlife Federation joins the Sierra Club and the Wilderness Society in calling for Watt's ouster.*

11/2/81 After a period of disarray, OPEC agrees on unified prices.

11/20/81 *EPA Administrator Anne Gorsuch plans even deeper budget cuts for her agency.*

11/25/81 *Most government agencies screech to a halt when Reagan vetoes a bill to keep the bureaucracy running while Congress hashes out Reaganomics.*

12/6/81 Unemployment hits a six-year high.

12/8/81 Reagan lifts ban on covert CIA activities in the United States.

21

12/10/81 The Louisiana and Arkansas legislatures pass bills requiring schools to teach "creation science" along with evolution. Both laws are later overturned.

"AND AS HE LOOKED BACK ON HIS FIRST YEAR IN OFFICE, THE PRESIDENT SAW THAT IT WAS GOOD."

12/24/81 Congress goes home just before Christmas, having enacted the Reagan Revolution.

1/13/82 Israelis raid Lebanese bases in southern Lebanon, killing innocent people.

2/3/82 *In his State of the Union Address, Reagan proposes to increase military spending and to transfer social programs to the states.*

2/11/82 Reagan's budget projects a $91.5 billion deficit, despite deep cuts in domestic spending.

"WELL... GUESS I'LL GO REASSURE THE PASSENGERS WITH THE OLD SMILE AND A FEW HOMILIES."

3/9/82 *Reagan defends his budget, promising, "We will not turn back . . . just as we near victory."*

27

3/12/82 Sen. Jesse Helms seeks to define life as beginning at conception. As usual, Sen. John East goes along for the ride.

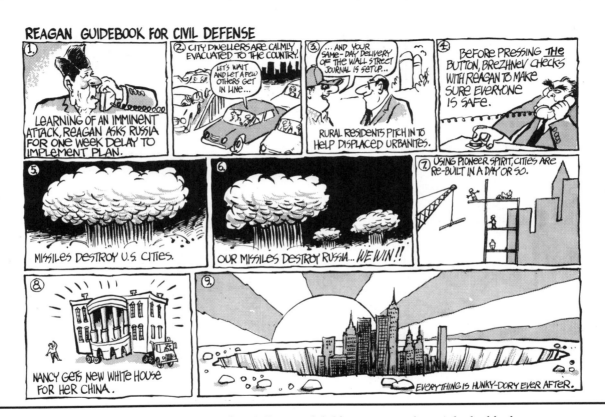

REAGAN GUIDEBOOK FOR CIVIL DEFENSE

4/2/82 *Reagan orders up a $4.2 billion civil defense program that might double the number of survivors of a nuclear attack—provided there was a week's notice.*

*5/6/82 Ann Landers admits recycling columns up to 15 years old.
A week later, her twin sister, Dear Abby, admits doing the same.*

5/17/82 *The budget debate, farmers, and the economy nose dive*
as reports surface of continued discontent among air traffic controllers.

5/24/82 ERA supporters stage a doomed, last-ditch rally as the June 30, 1982, deadline for ratification approaches.

9/29/82 The NFL strike drags on, with no progress reported in negotiations.

10/3/82 The administration tightens welfare eligibility rules; $1.5 billion in savings is projected over five years.

10/17/82 *Having slashed federal support for law enforcement,
Reagan proposes a crackdown on drug trafficking by organized crime.*

12/20/82 *Reagan claims executive privilege on cleaning up toxic waste dumps—and Anne Gorsuch gets a contempt citation for obeying orders.*

1/16/83 The Forest Service wants to give private industry a freer hand in national forests.

3/11/83 Anne Gorsuch Burford finally quits after the EPA agrees to fess up about its management of toxic waste dumps.

4/14/83 *Harold Washington is elected mayor of Chicago after a nasty campaign against Bernard Epton split the city along racial lines.*

5/24/83 *The Postal Service proposes to raise the price of first class stamps to 23 cents.*

6/30/83 Reagan tries a now-familiar defense when it is disclosed that his staff used "filched" material from the Carter campaign to prepare for the 1980 debate.

41

7/6/83 *The breakup of AT&T was intended to promote competition, but it isn't exactly improving service.*

7/9/83 More "debategate": It turns out that conservative pundit George Will coached Reagan prior to the 1980 debate, then praised his "game plan" on the air.

43

MILITARY SPARE PARTS CATALOGUE

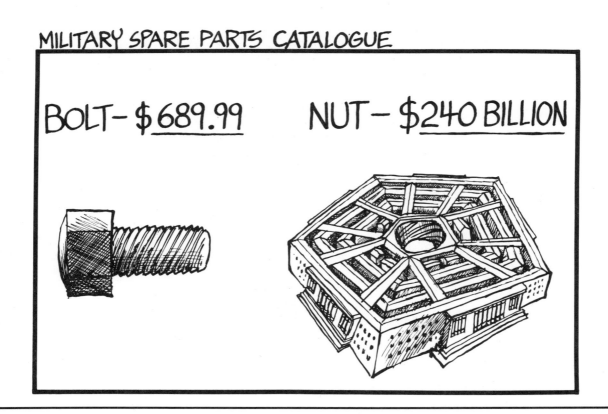

BOLT – $689.99

NUT – $240 BILLION

*7/28/83 As Reagan lobbies for spending nearly $240 billion for defense,
the GAO says the Pentagon has spent billions on "unproven" weapons.*

10/10/83 *Eastern Airlines President Frank Borman threatens to shut down the airline if the unions don't make more concessions.*

45

10/13/83 *Reagan slams Democrats as "big spenders" who should be the "last people" to "give sermonettes on fairness and compassion."*

10/14/83 When Watt quits after a flap over a tasteless joke, Reagan replaces him with William P. Clark, an old crony with practically no environmental record.

10/20/83 *Cabbage Patch Kids are so popular that stores run out in the middle of the Christmas season.*

10/24/83 When Nicaragua shoots down a rebel plane, reports surface
that the CIA is coordinating air operations in Honduras.

49

10/27/83 The United States scores a stunning military victory in Grenada.

12/14/83 Reagan gloats over Grenada as the U.S. death toll in Lebanon rises to 257.

"WE'VE ADVISED HIM NOT TO WORRY ABOUT THE DEFICIT AS A CAMPAIGN ISSUE – IT'S TOO ABSTRACT FOR MOST VOTERS TO COMPREHEND."

2/3/84 *The president presents a new budget with deficits in the $180 billion range through 1987.*

II.
THE AMAZING RON

2/14/84 Soviet leader Yuri Andropov dies after a brief stay in office and a protracted illness.

3/15/84 *A peculiar pattern emerges in Edwin Meese's confirmation hearings: People who do him financial favors keep turning up in government jobs.*

"J.B., YOU'RE A GREAT GUY! YOU GOT WORKERS TO TAKE A PAY CUT, THE COMPANY'S ROLLING IN PROFITS... HOW DOES A 6 MILLION BUCK BONUS SOUND? 'COULD YOU MAKE IT EIGHT?' AW, SURE, WHY NOT?..."

5/4/84 Companies blush when BusinessWeek *reports executive compensation and whopping raises—led by William Anderson's $13 million at NCR.*

5/15/84 *Soviet allies follow the USSR's lead when it pulls out of the Los Angeles Olympics.*

5/29/84 Walter Mondale's campaign is not exactly catching fire.

7/5/84 *Mondale comes under heavy pressure to select a woman as he interviews vice presidential candidates.*

*7/24/84 Vanessa Williams resigns as Miss America after reports that
nude pictures of her will appear in the September* Penthouse.

9/28/84 *There he goes again.*

10/22/84 George Bush used to think Reagan espoused "voodoo economics." Now he says the president's debate with Mondale "wrapped up four more years" and "laid to rest . . . attacks against our president's control of the facts."

63

10/31/84 Everyone in the administration is speaking for himself over whether to use military force against terrorists.

64

11/13/84 Pinochet cracks down on dissent in Chile; Reagan is "very disappointed."

12/14/84 *The election leaves the Democrats in disarray as they prepare for the next Congress.*

12/18/84 Reagan and Weinberger agree to $28.1 billion in defense cuts over three years—
less than half the amount proposed by OMB.

1/24/85 Tip O'Neill promises not to block votes on Reagan's policies, saying "there's a mandate out there demanding these things."

3/15/85 *"My veto pen is drawn and ready. . . . I have only one thing to say to the tax increasers: Go ahead and make my day."*

3/28/85 Reagan lobbies personally for funding for the MX missile—and eventually wins $1.5 billion to build 21 missiles.

70

5/15/85 After admissions of multimillion-dollar scams, the Justice Department decides not to prosecute individuals at E. F. Hutton and General Electric.

"WELL... DO WE UNDERSTAND REAGAN'S TAX SIMPLIFICATION PLAN?"

5/30/85 *Reagan barnstorms across the country to promote his plan to revise the federal tax code.*

6/18/85 Reagan discovers tough talk doesn't go very far after Shiites hijack a flight out of Athens and hold 40 Americans hostage.

73

6/23/85 *Complaining of "bias" at CBS News, Sen. Jesse Helms hatches a plan for a conservative buy-out.*

*7/7/85 Alleging an "ideological purge" in the State Department, Helms
leads a move to block diplomatic nominations and oust George Schultz.*

7/10/85 Reagan lashes out at "terrorist states" run by "misfits, Looney Tunes, and squalid criminals" — but doesn't say what he's going to do about them.

8/7/85 Major league players win concessions in a two-day strike, even though average salaries have risen to $360,000 from about half that figure in 1981.

8/28/85 *In the midst of a week of racial unrest in South Africa,*
Reagan asserts that Pretoria has "eliminated" segregation of public places.

"WE MOURN HIS PASSING BUT REJOICE THAT THROUGH HIS SACRIFICE OTHERS MAY SURVIVE AND FLOURISH...."

8/29/85 After spending $1.8 billion, the Pentagon abandons the Sergeant York mobile antiaircraft gun.
Reason: It couldn't hit anything.

79

FOLLOW THE BOUNCING BALL

$2,000,000,000,000 DEBT

9/17/85 The national debt reaches $2 trillion.

11/15/85 Jerry Falwell returns from South Africa and the Philippines, urging "unswerving support."

TOXIC DUMPS

*11/20/85 Two years after Reagan's confrontation with Congress over
toxic waste management, the EPA still hasn't cleaned up its act.*

12/5/85 Pentagon officials testify in Congress about the feasibility of Star Wars.

12/11/85 Congress relaxes federal handgun laws after heavy lobbying from the NRA.

12/15/85 *Congress passes Gramm-Rudman, requiring automatic budget cuts if the deficit is not brought under control.*

1/21/86 Reagan takes a dog-and-pony show to Grenada, where Prime Minister Herbert Blaize hails him as "our own national hero, our own rescuer, after God!"

2/6/86 Reagan's 1987 budget proposes to sell off federal assets to reduce the deficit. Congress is underwhelmed.

*3/2/86 Marcos flees in disgrace only hours after his inauguration—
and arrives in Hawaii with several million in cash and valuables.*

3/16/86 *In a high-pressure but unsuccessful bid to retain aid for the Nicaraguan rebels, Reagan declares, "I'm a contra, too."*

'WELL, HIGGINS, I SEE EVERYTHING'S UNDER CONTROL.'

3/18/86 *FAA Administrator Donald Engen casually dismisses a GAO survey showing that air traffic controllers are overworked.*

AFTER SIX MONTHS OF CAMPING IN THE ADIRONDACKS, GLADYS AND FRED FIND THAT THEY HAVE JUST ENTERED 'THE TWILIGHT ZONE.'

4/2/86 *OPEC discord sends gasoline prices plummeting by more than 25 cents since the beginning of the year.*

4/3/86 Out of government, Michael Deaver switches from peddling BMWs bought on diplomatic missions to peddling the B-1 for Rockwell International.

NOTED UROLOGIST DR. PETER VON SCHMEBLE THROWS OUT THE FIRST URINALYSIS BOTTLE.

4/8/86 Commissioner Peter Ueberroth clamps down on drugs in the major leagues.

4/22/86 *Reports of massive waste and inattention to safety emerge following the Challenger disaster.*

5/2/86 *The Soviet Union plays down the Chernobyl nuclear plant disaster while attacking the West for overemphasizing the crisis.*

5/27/86 CIA Director William Casey first goes after newspapers, then the White House itself in an effort to stanch leaks about the Ronald Pelton spy case.

96

5/28/86 *Chernobyl makes you wonder about the claims of the U.S. nuclear industry.*

6/10/86 *A presidential commission blames the Challenger disaster on NASA's carelessness. Military missions may now get priority.*

6/15/86 A barrage of contradictory statements by Reagan and others
leaves it unclear whether the president intends to abide by SALT II.

6/20/86 The AMA calls for lower medical school enrollments because of . . . gasp! . . . competition.

7/23/86 Fundamentalists in Tennessee challenge textbooks including readings from The Diary of Anne Frank *and* The Wizard of Oz—*and eventually win.*

7/29/86 *Consumer prices rise sharply as the economy stalls to the slowest pace since 1982.*

8/3/86 William Rehnquist's confirmation hearings for chief justice show that the jurist has a colorful past.

8/12/86 Reagan proposes mandatory drug testing for federal employees in sensitive posts.

8/21/86 After a drought so severe that Midwestern farmers sent hay to the Southeast, the region gets doused in August.

8/28/86 *The American Conservative Union may not know much about politics, but it knows what it likes.*

9/4/86 U.S. automakers go to unprecedented lengths to lure buyers away from imports.

107

9/5/86 Detention of journalist Nicholas Daniloff—apparently linked to the arrest of a Soviet physicist here—gives the lie to Gorbachev's "reforms."

10/8/86 After repeated denials, Reagan admits authorizing a "disinformation" campaign to make Qaddafi "go to bed every night wondering what we might do."

10/14/86 Reagan and Gorbachev leave Reykjavik without an arms deal after Reagan refuses to negotiate over Star Wars.

10/24/86 *Attorney General Edwin Meese pronounces that the rulings of the Supreme Court are not "the supreme law of the land."*

11/2/86 *A federal judge in Tennessee rules that schools may not require fundamentalists to study texts that violate their beliefs.*

III.
SWEEPING UP

11/7/86 "Iranamok" begins, as a secret U.S. arms deal with Iran is revealed.

11/18/86 Poindexter and North resign, but the Teflon seems to have melted.

11/25/86 Nancy is put out by the way her husband's top aides handled the Iran crisis.

11/30/86 After claiming he was "not informed" of the Iran scam, Reagan denies "flat out" any knowledge "whatsoever" of the transfer of funds to the contras.

12/5/86 Bush tries to distance himself from Iranscam as Reagan plummets
in the polls and North and Poindexter take the Fifth.

119

12/10/86 As more details emerge, Reagan admits that the "execution" of his
Iran policy was "flawed," but refuses to go further.

12/14/86 The Iran mess becomes an almost unbelievable tangle.

SEAL OF THE LT. COLONEL OF THE UNITED STATES · · ·

E PLURIBUS IMMUNITY

12/19/86 *Oliver North's superiors in the White House disavow knowledge of the Swiss bank accounts where the proceeds of the arms sales were deposited.*

UNWILLING TO USE STEROIDS TO COMPETE IN HIS LEAGUE, THE MAULERS' COACH RECRUITS HIS FATHER-IN-LAW'S 1958 BUICK.

GOLIATH

12/30/86 *Some two dozen college football players are banned after testing positive for steroids in a new testing program.*

123

1/9/87 The Pentagon seeks more money for the B-1, which can barely fly.

1/11/87 Reagan can't remember whether he authorized the Iran arms deal . . .

1/13/87 . . . *giving rise to doubts about his "detached" management style, only recently ballyhooed in* Fortune *magazine.*

2/17/87 Arbitrager Ivan Boesky and others go down in the insider trading scandal.

'GEE... I THINK I SENSE A SORT OF, ER, MALAISE.'

2/20/87 The mood in the administration recalls a Carter phrase as MacFarlane attempts suicide, Casey has a brain tumor, and North and Poindexter refuse to talk.

2/25/87 A "senior official" reports that Reagan is "unable to say with certainty whether he approved the first U.S.-sanctioned arms sales to Iran."

129

SCENE FROM TOWER COMMISSION REPORT

2/27/87 Initially, it appeared that Fawn Hall had shredded the documents and that Reagan had been detached from the Iran-contra affair.

3/4/87 Reagan appoints squeaky-clean Howard Baker as chief of staff.

3/25/87 Oral Roberts declares that God will take him home unless he receives millions in contributions, only to be saved by a greyhound track owner in Florida.

4/17/87 Reagan's policy wizards question Gorbachev's willingness to make a deal.

4/19/87 Scientists discover that living is hazardous to your health.

4/23/87 The Long Island garbage barge and Jim Bakker have difficulty finding a home.

4/28/87 Jim and Tammy mixed the Good News with the good life.

4/30/87 The PTL barge finds a home with the Rev. Jerry Falwell.

*5/6/87 In the '84 election it was discovered that Gary Hart had dropped
the "pence" from his born name of Hartpence; for '88 he dropped his pants.*

5/13/87 The U.S. was soliciting funds from third world governments to fund the contras.

5/15/87 As the hearings on the Iran-contra affair begin, the mighty Casey strikes out—just in time.

5/17/87 Falwell ups the ante to save the golden calf.

5/19/87 Iraq hits the Stark with an Exocet fired from a French-built fighter.

6/10/87 Fawn Hall testifies that she was only following orders and sometimes you have to "go above the law."

6/11/87 The best defense seems to be selling yourself as a "patriot."

6/21/87 *Lt. Col. Ollie North seems reluctant to cooperate with the Iran-Contra Committee.*

The next move is anybody's guess.